THE FONDUE COOKBOOK

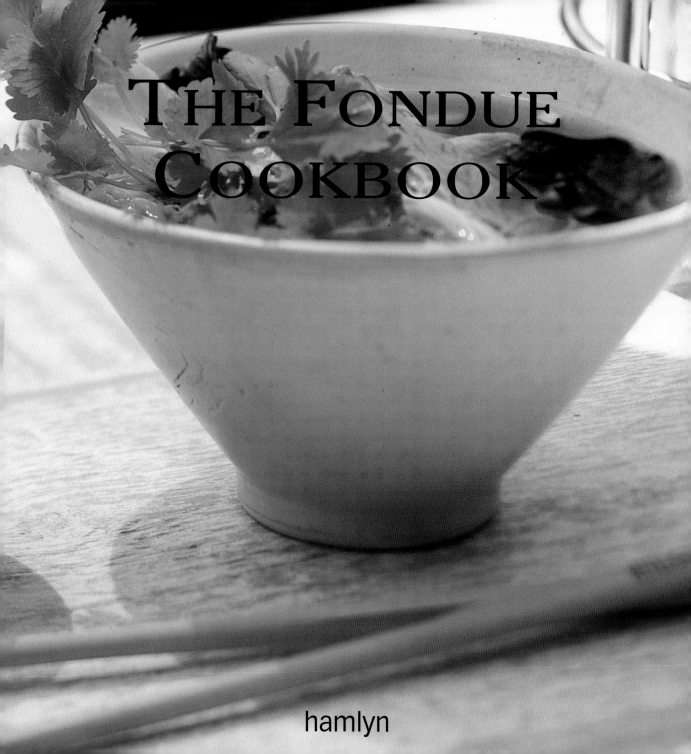

THE FONDUE
COOKBOOK

hamlyn

First published in 1999
by Hamlyn
a division of Octopus Publishing Group Limited
2–4 Heron Quays, London, E14 4JP

This edition published 2001

Distributed in the United States and Canada by
Sterling Publishing Co., Inc.
387 Park Avenue South, New York, NY 10016-8810

ISBN 0 600 60592 2

Printed in China

Photographer: Sean Myers
Home Economist: Louise Pickford

CONVERSION CHART

OVEN TEMPERATURES RECOMMENDED EQUIVALENTS			CONVERSIONS FROM CUPS TO IMPERIAL AND METRIC			
°C	°F	Gas Mark	Solid Measures		Terminology	
110	225	¼	**American**	**Imperial and Metric**	**American**	**English**
120	250	½	1 cup butter	8 oz/250 g	All-purpose Flour	Plain Flour
140	275	1	4 cups flour	1 lb/500 g	Cilantro	Coriander
150	300	2	2 cups granulated or caster sugar	1 lb/500 g	Confectioners' Sugar	Icing Sugar
160	325	3	3 cups icing sugar	1 lb/500 g	Cornstarch	Cornflour
180	350	4	1 cup rice	8 oz/250 g	Eggplant	Aubergine
190	375	5	½ cup cornflour	3 oz/75 g	Green/Red Bell Pepper	Green/Red Pepper
200	400	6			Green Onion (Scallion)	Spring Onion
220	425	7	Liquid Measures		Golden Raisins	Sultanas
230	450	8	**American**	**Imperial and Metric**	Ground Beef	Minced Beef
240	475	9	⅔ cup	¼ pint/150 ml	Heavy Cream	Double Cream
			1¼ cups	½ pint/300 ml	Light Cream	Single Cream
			2 cups	¾ pint/450 ml	Self-rising Flour	Self-raising Flour
			2½ cups	1 pint/600 ml	Semi-sweet Chocolate	Plain Chocolate
			3¾ cups	1½ pints/900 ml	Shrimp	Prawn
			5 cups	2 pints/1200 ml	Snow Peas	Mangetout
					Zucchini	Courgette

Notes 1 Use whole milk unless otherwise stated. 2 Keep meat refrigerated until ready for cooking.
3 Cooking times based on stovetop cooking and not the total tabletop cooking unless otherwise stated.

Contents

THE FONDUE COOKBOOK

When you think of flavorful and convivial tabletop dining, fondues immediately spring to mind. The word fondue comes from the French *fondre*, meaning "to melt" or "to blend," as originally this Swiss national dish was made with cheese melted in wine. Fondues have recently had a resurgence of interest, and it's easy to see why. A fondue is an easy and often inexpensive dish to serve at a casual lunch or dinner party, where it can be used either as a main course or a dessert (or even both). Sauces and accompaniments can be as few or as many as liked. Since most of the preparation can be done in advance, you can have more time to spend with your guests. And because so many ingredients lend themselves to fondue-making, you can create a diverse range of dishes, both savory and sweet.

History and Traditions

There are many stories about the origin of fondues, but the one most commonly told concerns isolated villagers who, during a long, harsh winter, subsisted on what was on hand—cheese (that hardened), home-made bread (that became stale), and wine. They christened the dish *fondue au fromage*. The first fondues were made with Emmentaler cheese (also called Emmental or Emmenthal) and Swiss Gruyère and were cooked in a thick, earthenware pan called a *caquelon*, which ensured that the cheese melted slowly and did not become lumpy or stringy. The creamy mixture was eaten with skewered pieces of French bread. Later, other dishes were derived from the traditional cheese fondue: including fondue *bourguignonne* (from the French beef *bourguignonne* from Burgundy), a meat- (but also poultry-, fish-, and vegetable-) based fondue that is cooked in stock or in hot oil, and dessert fondues, which are often made with chocolate and liqueur.

The Chinese also have their own version of fondue. Introduced to the Far East by the Mongols in the fourteenth century, their fondue was originally made with mutton, *bourguignonne*-style, in a fondue pot over a charcoal burner that is incorporated into it. Nowadays strips of meat (beef and pork), slices of chicken breast, pieces of fish, and chicken stock are used.

There are a number of traditions associated with eating a fondue. The Swiss prefer to drink Kirsch or Chasselas, a white wine, with their cheese fondues, and share among all the guests the delicious cheese crust that is left in the pan. They then serve sausages and crisp apples or pears for their next course! Another Swiss custom is the forfeit: if a woman drops a cube of bread into the fondue, she has to kiss all the men; if a man drops the bread cube, he has to buy a bottle of wine for each guest. And if the person drops a cube of bread for a second time, he or she must host the next fondue party.

Equipment

There are different types of fondue pots, and it is important to use the correct one for your chosen dish. Alternatively, if you only want to buy a single pot, choose one that is made of stainless steel or copper with a removable porcelain insert. The fondue pot *with* the insert can be used for cheese or chocolate fondues; the fondue pot *without* the insert can be used for the fondue *bourguignonne* and its variations.

Pots for cheese fondues

These are either made of glazed earthenware, or ceramic-lined metal, or metal (stainless steel or copper) with a porcelain insert, or cast iron. These pots are thick, heavy, and shallow, and their slow transmission of heat helps prevent the cheese from burning too fast.

Pots for meat, poultry, fish, and vegetable fondues

These are usually metal (stainless steel or copper) or cast iron and are larger than cheese-fondue pots. The metal transmits heat quickly and helps keep the cooking liquid at a high temperature.

Pots for dessert fondues

These are stainless steel and copper and should have a porcelain insert.

Many fondue pots are sold as boxed sets, which include a stand, a burner, long, two-pronged metal skewers (often with colored handles so diners know which one is theirs), and sometimes a cork mat to go under the stand to protect the table. Depending upon the type of burner you have, you can use solid sterno in packets that are made to fit into the burner, or alcohol for fuel. Electric fondue pots are also available. Always read and follow the manufacturer's instructions for preparing and caring for your fondue pot so that it will last for many years.

Cheese fondues

Cheeses have different fat and moisture levels, and therefore react differently to heat, so it is important to choose the correct type of cheese for this dish. Use a cheese or combination of cheeses that is good for melting, and yields a smooth and creamy consistency. The best cheeses are Emmentaler, Swiss Gruyère, Swiss, Fontina, Pecorino, Provolone, Parmesan, Vacherin, Gouda, Edam, and Cheddar. However, many other cheeses have been used in fondue recipes, including mature Comté, Appenzell, Bagnes, Tilsit, Beaufort, Camembert, Pont l'Evêque, and Livarot, to name a few. If you use a low-fat-content cheese, you may need to add a knob of butter to the mixture to prevent the cheese from sticking to the pot. Always use an aged (mature) cheese: if the cheese is not aged or is poorly aged it won't melt smoothly.

Heat is vital, too: if it is too intense, the cheese will become stringy and the fondue will be spoiled. The heat must also be carefully controlled; this is easily done by adjusting the heat control on the burner.

It is traditional to rub the inside of the pot with a piece of cut garlic before adding the wine. As the cheese melts in the hot wine, try adding a little lemon juice; its acidity will help to melt the cheese completely. You can also add some Kirsch, mixed with a little cornflour as a thickener and stabilizer. Stir the fondue with a wooden spoon, using a figure eight motion, for a smooth blend. When the pot is set over the burner, adjust the heat so that the fondue bubbles gently. Never rush a cheese fondue as slow cooking gives the best results.

If the fondue becomes too thick, add a little warmed wine; if too thin, add a little cornstarch. If the fondue separates and becomes lumpy, place the pot on the stovetop over a moderate heat and whisk gently. Blend a little cornstarch with a little wine and stir gently into the fondue.

Dry white wine is nearly always used for the cheese fondues, with Kirsch, beer, and Champagne as tasty alternatives in some recipes.

French bread is the traditional dipper for all cheese fondues. If the crust is kept on and the bread is one-day old, spearing will be easier. Other breads to use include pita, grissini, brown or rye bread cubes, or indeed any bread that would complement the dish. However, it is not necessary to limit yourself to bread: many recipes call for shrimp, salami, or sausage, or for a lighter meal raw vegetables. Sauces are unnecessary, but if you like you can accompany this fondue with a salad of greens such as Belgian endive, peppery arugula, or watercress.

Kirsch and Chasselas are the drinks of choice for the Swiss (with tea as an alternative), but you don't have to follow this example. Wine is one of the more popular options. The best are dry white wines such as *premier cru* Chablis, Hock, or Riesling, or a California Chardonnay or New World Sauvignon. For a really wonderful variation, try the red Chinon.

Beer makes a good accompaniment to a beer and cheese fondue and, for a special occasion, Champagne for a Champagne and cheese fondue (see pages 32–3).

Meat, poultry, fish, and vegetable fondues

Meat and chicken fondues

It is best to heat the cooking liquid on the stovetop before bringing the fondue pot to the table. For oil, the temperature needs to be 350–375°F, or when a cube of bread carefully placed in the oil browns in 30 seconds. The stock should be boiling.

The best cuts of meat make for a more tender, flavorful, and quickly cooked meat fondue. Fillet or sirloin steak is the basis for the traditional *bourguignonne*, but pork and lamb fillet make tasty alternatives. These meats can either be cut into bite-sized pieces or into slices (see the tip for slicing meat in Mongolian Lamb Hot Pot on page 42). If you like, you can marinate the meat first for extra flavor. You can also make a novel fondue with meat-balls (see page 48).

Do not let meat or poultry fall to the bottom of the pot as it can stick. And don't over-fill the pot or the oil will froth up and overflow.

The tastiest and most tender poultry to use is skinned breast meat. The meat can either be sliced thinly into strips or slivers or cut into bite-sized pieces.

The liquid for these two fondues is usually chicken stock, but depending on the dish, consommé and even coconut milk (for a Thai fondue) can be used.

Meat fondues especially, but also poultry, can be enlivened with sauces, relishes, chutneys, mayonnaises, mustards, and ketchups. The recipes in this book do suggest a selection of go-alongs, but you can prepare many others that will make good partners with your chosen ingredients. Chinese fondues can be made into a real feast with the addition of rice or noodles, and even spring rolls (see page 46).

For a rich meat-based fondue such as a Fondue *Bourguignonne* (see page 50), offer a full red wine such as California or Coonawarra Cabernet, or a Burgundy or Bordeaux. White or red wines both go well with poultry. The more basic dishes can have a French *vin de pays*, going up the scale to an oaked Chardonnay, and onto reds like Bergerac.

Fish fondues

Firm fish and shellfish are best for fish fondues, although flaked fish such as crab will add a delicate touch to the dish. Flat fish need to be boned and the skin removed before being cut into bite-sized pieces. Shrimp should be peeled, mussels shelled, and squid cleaned and cut into bite-sized pieces. Dry white wine is very good for fish fondues; a dash of brandy adds another level of flavor. Oil is used for deep-frying.

Fish fondues are often lighter, with the shellfish such as shrimp and mussels used as a dipper. French and pita breads are other alternatives, as are cheese straws and puff pastry crescents. Tartar sauce and a salad would complete the meal.

Shellfish fondues will benefit from wines that are crisp, dry, and white, such as a Muscadet sur lie, Chablis, New World Sauvignon Blanc, or an unoaked or lightly oaked Chardonnay.

Vegetable fondues

Almost any vegetable can be used for a fondue, but it is best to choose those that can be eaten in one or two bites. If baby vegetables are unavailable, use whole vegetables (button mushrooms, shallots, snow peas, radishes) or cut them into thin strips or sticks (carrots, celery), slices (zucchini), pieces (asparagus tips or spears), and florets (broccoli, cauliflower).

Vegetables can make up the fondue itself or be used as dippers. Or you can follow serving suggestions for a cheese fondue, such as salami, or corn chips. For a treat, try the sauce that accompanies Tempura (see page 30).

White wine is perfect for vegetable fondues. Try one that is crisp, dry, and aromatic such as an Australian Riesling or a Vouvray.

Dessert fondues

When preparing a chocolate fondue, always follow the recipe directions. It may be necessary to put water into the fondue pot under the insert before it is placed on the burner, thereby creating a water bath (*bain-marie*) which prevents the chocolate from burning. Dessert fondues can be cooked in liqueurs, juices, and cream.

Although chocolate and orange are classic partners, almost any fruit can be used in these fondues. Chunks of banana, pineapple, peach, kiwis, nectarine, and plum, and whole raspberries, strawberries, and cherries are all delicious. These fondues can also be served with plain biscuits, macaroons, cookies, lady fingers, pound cake and marshmallows.

Dessert wines and liqueurs are preferable with these fondues. If one of them is used in the fondue itself, you can serve it, for example on the rocks, with the dish.

Party planning

Fondue parties work best if there are no more than six people at the table as a fondue pot only holds a certain amount of food. However, for a fondue buffet, you can borrow a second pot and make two different fondues, one meat and one vegetable, for example. Advise guests that food from the pot is very hot, and that they should not eat it immediately from the skewers or they'll burn their tongues.

For advance preparation, cut the bread into chunks and pile it in baskets, and set out the dippers and sauces in separate bowls on the table. For a Chinese fondue, you'll need soup bowls and spoons to drink the stock, and perhaps chopsticks. For dessert fondues with fruit, prepare the fruit just before the party begins, squeeze over some lemon juice to prevent the fruit from turning brown, and heap into serving bowls.

TRADITIONAL CHEESE FONDUE (NEUCHÂTEL FONDUE)

1 garlic clove
⅔ cup dry white wine
1 teaspoon lemon juice
10 ounces Emmentaler cheese, grated
10 ounces Gruyère cheese, grated
1 tablespoon cornstarch
3 tablespoons Kirsch
pinch of white pepper
pinch of ground nutmeg
pinch of paprika
cubes of French bread, to serve

1 Rub the inside of a fondue pot with the cut clove of garlic, then discard the garlic. Pour the wine into the pot with the lemon juice and heat gently on the stove. Gradually add the cheese, stirring in a figure eight motion, until all the cheese is combined.

2 Blend the cornstarch and Kirsch together and as soon as the cheese mixture begins to bubble, add to the fondue. Continue to cook gently for a further 2–3 minutes and season, according to taste, with the pepper, nutmeg, and paprika.

3 Transfer the fondue pot to the table and keep warm on a burner. Serve with cubes of French bread to dip into the fondue.

Serves 4
Preparation time: 10 minutes
Cooking time: 15–20 minutes

GORGONZOLA CHEESE FONDUE

2 cups grated or crumbled Gorgonzola or
other blue cheese
2 cups grated Gruyère cheese
3 tablespoons all-purpose flour
1 cup dry white wine
1 garlic clove, crushed
⅓ cup Kirsch
pinch of nutmeg
pepper

To serve:
cubes of toasted bread
stalks of celery, trimmed
slices of carrot
spears of endive

1 Mix the cheeses with the flour. Heat the wine and garlic in a fondue pot on the stove.

2 Add the cheese gradually, stirring continuously and allowing each amount to melt before adding more. When all the cheese has been added and the mixture is smooth, stir in the Kirsch, nutmeg, and pepper to taste.

3 Transfer the fondue pot to the table and keep warm on a burner. Serve with cubes of toasted bread, stalks of celery, carrot, and spears of endive to dip into the fondue.

Serves 4
Preparation time: 15 minutes
Cooking time: 15–20 minutes

THREE CHEESE FONDUE

1 garlic clove
4 tablespoons butter
1–2 stalks of celery, finely chopped
1¼ cups dry white wine
12 ounces Emmentaler cheese, grated
12 ounces Gruyère cheese, grated
⅔ cup grated Parmesan cheese
pinch of dried mustard
pinch of nutmeg
pinch of cayenne pepper
3 teaspoons cornstarch
2 tablespoons brandy

To serve:
peeled jumbo shrimp
cubes of brown or French bread

1 Rub the inside of the fondue pot with the cut clove of garlic, then discard the garlic. Add the butter and cook over a medium heat on the stove until it melts. Fry the celery for 5–10 minutes. Stir in the wine and heat gently.

2 Gradually add the cheeses, stirring until melted. Season with the mustard, nutmeg, and cayenne pepper. Blend the cornstarch with the brandy and add to the fondue. Bring to the boil and cook for 10 minutes, stirring constantly.

3 Transfer the fondue pot to the table and keep warm on a burner. Serve with peeled shrimp and cubes of brown or French bread to dip into the fondue.

Serves 4
Preparation time: 10–15 minutes
Cooking time: 30–40 minutes

DUTCH FONDUE

Many years ago, the farmers' wives in Holland used the cheeses which were not perfect in shape for making fondue. Dutch gin was generally used for flavoring, but in this recipe, Kirsch, whiskey, brandy, or sherry could be used.

½ **garlic clove**
⅔ **cup dry white wine**
I **teaspoon lemon juice**
3½ **cups grated Gouda or Edam cheese**
I **tablespoon cornstarch**
1½ **tablespoons gin**
black pepper
pinch of nutmeg
cubes of French bread, to serve

I Rub the inside of the fondue pot with the cut garlic, then discard the garlic. Pour in the wine and lemon juice and heat slowly on the stove until the wine is nearly boiling. Add the cheese a little at a time, stirring continuously, until all the cheese has melted.

2 Blend the cornstarch smoothly with the gin and when the cheese mixture boils, stir in the blended cornstarch.

3 Add a dash of black pepper and the nutmeg.

4 Transfer the fondue pot to the table and keep warm on a burner. Serve with cubes of French bread for dipping into the fondue and, if liked, accompany with a tossed green salad.

Serves 4
Preparation time: 10 minutes
Cooking time: 20 minutes

ITALIAN FONDUE

One of the Italian cheeses such as Pecorino or Provolone should be used in this fondue. Pecorino cheeses are made from ewe's milk and a great deal is exported. Provolone cheese comes in a variety of shapes and has a strong flavor. If neither is available, use Parmesan.

1 garlic clove
1¼ cups dry white wine
1 teaspoon lemon juice
5 cups grated Provolone, Pecorino, or Parmesan cheese
2 tablespoons cornstarch
4 tablespoons Kirsch or sherry
cubes of Italian bread, to serve

1 Rub the inside of the fondue pot with the cut clove of garlic, then discard the garlic. Add the wine and lemon juice and warm over a low heat on the stove.

2 Add the cheese gradually and stir until it has melted, keeping the heat low. Mix the cornstarch smoothly with the Kirsch, add to the cheese mixture, and stir in a figure eight motion until the fondue bubbles and is thick and creamy.

3 Transfer the fondue pot to the table and keep warm on a burner. Serve with cubes of Italian bread to dip into the fondue.

Serves 4–5
Preparation time: 10 minutes
Cooking time: about 20 minutes

FRESH HERB FONDUE

1 garlic clove
⅔ cup dry white wine
1 pound **Gruyère cheese**, grated
3 teaspoons cornstarch
1 tablespoon chopped parsley
1 tablespoon chopped chives
1 tablespoon chopped oregano
salt and pepper

To serve:
cubes of French bread
cubes of salami sausage

1 Rub the inside of a fondue pot with the cut clove of garlic, then discard the garlic. Pour in the wine, and heat gently, then add the cheese. Stir continuously, until melted. Blend the cornstarch with a little water and add to the fondue with the herbs, and salt and pepper to taste. Heat until thickened, stirring well.

2 Transfer the fondue pot to the table and keep warm on a burner. Serve with cubes of French bread and cubes of salami sausage to dip into the fondue.

Serves 4
Preparation time: 10 minutes
Cooking time: 15 minutes

GENEVA FONDUE

This is a rich, thin fondue generally eaten with noodles. Have them cooked and kept hot while the fondue is being made.

8 egg yolks
8 ounces Gruyère cheese, grated
a little grated nutmeg
½ cup butter
⅔ cup heavy cream
salt and pepper
cooked noodles, to serve

1 Beat the egg yolks and put them into the fondue pot with the cheese, nutmeg, and salt and pepper to taste.

2 Place the pot over a gentle heat on the stove and stir until the cheese has melted, then add the butter a little at a time, stirring continuously over a gentle heat.

3 When the mixture thickens, add the cream. Stir for a few minutes longer then pour over the noodles.

Serves 3–4
Preparation time: 10 minutes
Cooking time: 20 minutes

BERNESE FONDUE

This fondue generally contains a mixture of cheeses including Sbrinz, probably the oldest Swiss hard cheese, from the South Central Alps region. It is not generally exported, and the Sbrinz cheese sold in America usually comes from Argentina and is really a variety of Parmesan.

1 garlic clove
4 tablespoons butter
2–3 shallots, peeled
1 cup button mushrooms
½ bottle dry white wine
3 cups grated Emmentaler cheese
3 cups grated Gruyère cheese
⅔ cup grated Parmesan or Sbrinz cheese
¼ teaspoon dried mustard
¼ teaspoon paprika
¼ teaspoon grated nutmeg
3 teaspoons cornstarch
2 tablespoons sherry
salt and pepper
cubes of French bread, to serve

1 Rub the cut clove of garlic round the inside of the fondue pot, then discard the garlic. Add the butter and when it has melted add the shallots and mushrooms. Cook for 5–10 minutes.

2 Stir in the white wine and when hot, but not boiling, add the cheeses and stir continuously until melted. Add the mustard, paprika, and nutmeg, and season with salt and pepper.

3 Add the cornstarch blended smoothly with the sherry. Stir until almost boiling then simmer for about 15 minutes, stirring constantly in a figure eight motion. Serve with cubes of French bread to dip into the fondue.

Serves 4–5
Preparation time: 10 minutes
Cooking time: about 30 minutes

AVOCADO FONDUE

2 tablespoons butter
1 onion, finely chopped
4 tablespoons all-purpose flour
1 cup milk
4 tablespoons lemon juice
1 avocado, mashed or blended (skin and pit removed)
1 cup grated Swiss cheese
⅔ cup cream
few drops of Tabasco sauce
salt and pepper

1 Gently melt the butter in a fondue pot on the stove. Add the onion and sauté until softened. Stir in the flour and cook for 2 minutes. Remove from the heat and add the milk, lemon juice, and avocado. Season to taste with salt and pepper.

2 Cook gently for 5 minutes, stirring constantly, taking care not to boil the mixture. Add the cheese and stir until melted. Stir in the cream and Tabasco sauce.

3 Transfer the fondue pot to the table and keep warm on a burner. Serve immediately with cherry tomatoes with their vines attached for dipping, cubes of French bread, and peeled shrimp to dip into the fondue.

To serve:
cherry or vine tomatoes
cubes of French bread
cooked and peeled shrimp

Serves 4
Preparation time: 10 minutes
Cooking time: 20–25 minutes

ONION AND CARAWAY FONDUE

If you find the flavor of caraway seeds too strong, then try using fennel seeds or lightly toasted sesame seeds instead.

4 tablespoons butter
2 cups chopped onions
2 teaspoons caraway seeds
1¼ cups dry white wine
3 cups grated Gruyère cheese
3 cups grated Emmentaler cheese
1 teaspoon wholegrain mustard
pinch of ground nutmeg
1 tablespoon cornstarch
2 tablespoons dry vermouth
cubes of French bread, to serve

1 Melt the butter in a fondue pot on the stove and sauté the onions and caraway seeds for 5–10 minutes, until they are soft but not browned.

2 Pour in the wine and heat gently. Gradually add the cheeses, stirring continuously until melted. Add the mustard and nutmeg.

3 Blend the cornstarch with the vermouth and stir into the fondue. Cook over a low heat, stirring continuously until thickened.

4 Transfer the fondue pot to the table and keep warm on a burner. Serve with cubes of bread to dip into the fondue.

Serves 4–6
Preparation time: 15–20 minutes
Cooking time: 25–30 minutes

SPRING VEGETABLE FONDUE

16 button mushrooms
16 cauliflower florets
16 broccoli florets
16 carrot sticks
16 tiny par-boiled potatoes
16 zucchini slices
vegetable oil, for frying

Batter:
scant 1 cup all-purpose flour, sifted
½ teaspoon salt
1 tablespoon corn oil
⅔ cup water
2 egg whites

To serve:
Tomato relish (see below) or selection of
dipping sauces (see page 50)

1 Make sure the vegetables are cut into small pieces, so that they will cook quickly. Wash and pat dry with paper towels to remove any excess moisture.

2 To prepare the batter, mix the flour and salt together in a bowl and gradually add the oil and water, beating until smooth. Whisk the egg whites until forming stiff peaks and carefully fold into the batter, just before required.

3 Half-fill a pot with oil and heat on the stove to 350°F, or until a cube of bread browns in 30 seconds.

4 Carefully transfer the oil to the fondue and keep hot on a fondue burner. Spear pieces of vegetable onto fondue forks and dip into the batter, coating well. Cook in the oil until the batter is crisp and golden brown.

5 Serve with a selection of sauces such as Tomato Relish, or garlic mayonnaise, a mixed salad, and French bread.

Serves 4
Preparation time: about 30 minutes
Cooking time: 5–10 minutes

TOMATO RELISH

6 ripe tomatoes, skinned
and chopped
6 red bell peppers, cored, deseeded and
finely chopped
3 large onions, finely chopped
2 red chiles, deseeded and finely chopped
1¾ cups red wine vinegar
¾ cup packed brown sugar
4 tablespoons mustard seeds
2 tablespoons celery seeds
1 tablespoon paprika
2 teaspoons salt
2 teaspoons pepper

1 Place all the ingredients in a large pan and slowly bring to the boil. Simmer, uncovered, for about 30 minutes until most of the liquid has evaporated and the relish is of a thick, pulpy consistency. Stir frequently as the relish thickens.

2 Pour into clean, sterilized jars. To sterilize the jars, put the clean jars open end up on a baking sheet and place in a preheated cool oven, 275°F, for about 10 minutes until hot. Seal with vinegar-proof covers, once cool.

Makes about 3 pounds
Preparation time: 20 minutes
Cooking time: about 35 minutes

BAGNA CAUDA WITH SUMMER VEGETABLES

This is a classic warm oil, butter, and anchovy dip found all over Italy and is the perfect accompaniment to your favorite sweet fragrant summer vegetables.

2 tablespoons unsalted butter
2 garlic cloves, crushed
½ of a 2-ounce can anchovies in oil, drained
½ cup olive oil
I pound prepared summer vegetables (such as baby carrots, radishes, topped and tailed green beans, asparagus, stalks of celery, etc.)
French bread, to serve

1 Place the butter and garlic in a small saucepan or earthenware fondue pot and heat gently until the butter is melted. Simmer gently for 2 minutes but do not allow the butter or garlic to burn.
2 Stir in the anchovies and then gradually whisk in the oil. Continue to heat gently for 10 minutes, stirring constantly.
3 Pour into a heatproof bowl, or leave in the fondue pot, and serve at once with a selection of vegetable crudités and some crusty French bread to dunk into the fondue.

Serves 4–6
Preparation time: 10 minutes, plus preparing vegetables
Cooking time: about 20 minutes

ASPARAGUS AND BLUE CHEESE FONDUE

8–10 asparagus stalks
2 cups crumbled blue cheese
1 heaped tablespoon all-purpose flour
⅔ cup dry white wine
⅔ cup light cream
pepper

To serve:
cubes of ham
cubes of French bread
slices of salami

1 Trim away any woody bases from the asparagus and peel if necessary. Cook in boiling salted water for 10–15 minutes until tender. Drain and chop into ½-inch pieces.

2 Mix the cheese and flour together. Heat the wine in a fondue pot until almost boiling. Add the cheese and flour mixture and stir continuously until thickened. Stir in the cream and season with pepper, then add the asparagus and heat gently for 3–4 minutes.

3 Transfer the fondue pot to the table and keep warm on a burner. Serve with cubes of ham and bread, and slices of salami to dip into the fondue.

Serves 4
Preparation time: 10 minutes
Cooking time: 30–35 minutes

BLUE CHEESE AND CHIVE FONDUE

1 garlic clove, halved
1 tablespoon cornstarch
⅔ cup white wine
8 ounces Stilton or Danish blue cheese, crumbled
1¼ cups sour cream
1 tablespoon chopped parsley
3 tablespoons chopped chives
salt and pepper

To serve:
12 red-skinned (new) potatoes, boiled and halved
2 cups broccoli florets
2 cups cauliflower florets

1 Rub the inside of an earthenware fondue pot with the cut clove of garlic, then discard the garlic.

2 Blend the cornstarch with a little of the wine, add the remaining wine to the fondue pot, and bring to the boil. Add the cornstarch mixture and cook, stirring constantly, until thickened.

3 Add the cheese and stir until melted, then add the sour cream, parsley, chives, and salt and pepper to taste.

4 Transfer the fondue pot to the table and keep warm on a burner. Serve with potatoes and broccoli and cauliflower florets to dip into the fondue.

Serves 4–6
Preparation time: 10–15 minutes
Cooking time: 20 minutes

TEMPURA

sunflower oil, for deep-frying
8 asparagus stalks, trimmed
1 red bell pepper, cored, deseeded and
sliced lengthways into strips
4 zucchini, sliced into rounds

Batter:
1 cup all-purpose flour
2 tablespoons arrowroot or cornstarch
pinch of salt
1¼ cups of iced water

Dipping sauce:
4 tablespoons soy sauce
4 tablespoons dry sherry
1 tablespoon finely chopped fresh
ginger root
pinch of dried mustard
½ teaspoon sugar

1 First make the batter. Sift the all-purpose flour, and arrowroot or cornstarch into a bowl with the salt. Add the water a little at a time, whisking constantly. Cover and place in the refrigerator to chill for 30 minutes.

2 Meanwhile, whisk the dipping sauce ingredients together in a bowl. Pour enough oil into a saucepan or a fondue pot for deep-frying and heat on the stove to 375°F, or until a cube of bread browns in 30 seconds.

3 Using a slotted spoon, dip a few pieces of each vegetable into the batter, then lift them out, making sure there is plenty of batter around them.

4 Transfer the fondue pot to the table and keep the oil hot on a burner. Lower the vegetables gently into the hot oil and deep-fry for 2–3 minutes until crisp. Lift out with a slotted spoon, drain on paper towels and keep hot while deep-frying the remainder.

5 Whisk the dipping sauce again before serving, then divide equally between individual dipping bowls.

Serves 4
Preparation time: 10 minutes
Cooking time: 2–3 minutes for each batch

CHAMPAGNE FONDUE

I cup mushroom caps
2 cups Champagne
4 cups grated Swiss cheese
¾ cup all-purpose flour
2 egg yolks
I tablespoon cream
salt and pepper

To serve:
cubes of ham
cubes of French bread
cubes of cucumber

1 To prepare the mushrooms, cook for 5 minutes in enough boiling water to just cover. Drain, reserving ¼ cup of the cooking liquid and slice the mushrooms thinly.

2 Heat the Champagne slowly in a fondue pot on the stove. Stir in the cheese and flour, and cook, stirring until melted and smooth.

3 Combine the egg yolks, cream, the reserved mushroom liquid, and the mushrooms and stir into the fondue. Do not allow to boil. Season with salt and pepper to taste.

4 Transfer the fondue pot to the table and keep hot on a burner. Serve with cubes of ham, French bread, and cucumber to dip into the fondue.

Serves 4
Preparation time: 20 minutes
Cooking time: about 25 minutes

BEER AND ONION FONDUE

3 tablespoons butter
1 finely chopped onion
1 cup beer
2 cups grated Cheddar cheese
1 garlic clove, crushed
3 tablespoons cornstarch
½ teaspoon dried mustard
pepper

To serve:
cubes of French bread
pickled onions

1 Heat 1 tablespoon of the butter in a skillet. Add the onion and gently fry until softened but not browned.

2 Place the beer, cheese, crushed garlic, and onion in a fondue pot. Cook gently, stirring, over a low heat on the stove until the cheese has melted. Stir in the remaining butter.

3 Blend the cornstarch and mustard in a little water and add to the fondue pot. Continue cooking until thickened, stirring constantly. Season with pepper to taste.

4 Transfer the fondue pot to the table and keep hot on a burner. Serve with cubes of French bread and pickled onions to dip into the fondue.

Serves 2
Preparation time: 10 minutes
Cooking time: about 20 minutes

CHILI CON QUESO

To make the fried tortillas, cut 4–6 flour tortillas into thin triangles. Fry in a heavy saucepan filled with hot oil for about 30–60 seconds, or until crisp.

2 tablespoons butter
½ cup chopped onions
1–2 garlic cloves, minced
2–4 green or red chiles, seeded and chopped
3–4 tablespoons jalapeños, chopped and seeded (canned or fresh)
1¼ cups peeled, seeded and chopped tomatoes
½ cup cream cheese, cut into cubes
2 cups grated Cheddar cheese
salt
milk or light cream (optional)
fried flour tortillas (see above) or blue corn chips, to serve

1 Melt the butter in a heavy saucepan or fondue pot. Add the onions and garlic and cook gently, stirring occasionally, until softened. Add the chiles, adjusting quantity according to taste, jalapeños, and tomatoes. Cook, stirring constantly, until the excess liquid has evaporated.

2 Add both cheeses and cook very gently, stirring, until they have melted. Do not let the mixture get too hot. Add salt to taste.

3 Transfer the fondue to an earthenware dish or keep in the fondue pot and keep hot on a burner.

4 If the dip becomes too thick, stir in a little milk or cream. Serve with fried tortillas or blue corn chips to dip into the fondue.

Serves 6–8
Preparation time: 10–15 minutes
Cooking time: about 30 minutes

SMOKED HADDOCK FONDUE

1½ pounds smoked haddock fillet
1 small onion, chopped
1 carrot, sliced
1 bouquet garni
5 peppercorns
small handful of parsley, chopped
1¼ cups white wine
salt and pepper

To serve:
tartar sauce
pita bread
green salad

1 Skin the haddock. Cut it into bite-sized chunks and put to one side. Place the fish trimmings in a saucepan with the onion, carrot, bouquet garni, peppercorns, and parsley. Cover with cold water and bring to the boil, then simmer for 30 minutes. Strain, season with salt and pepper and add the wine.

2 Pour the mixture into a fondue pot and bring to the boil. Transfer the fondue pot to the table and keep hot on a burner.

3 To eat, spear a chunk of haddock onto a fondue fork and dip into the boiling stock until cooked. Serve with tartar sauce, pita bread, and a green salad.

Serves 4
Preparation time: 15 minutes
Cooking time: 35 minutes

SHRIMP AND CHEESE FONDUE

1 garlic clove
2 tablespoons butter
2 shallots, chopped
1 cup mushrooms, finely chopped
⅔ cup dry white wine
1½ cups grated Swiss cheese
1½ cups grated Cheddar cheese
3 teaspoons cornstarch
2 tablespoons brandy
1 cup cooked and peeled shrimp
4 tablespoons light cream
salt and pepper

To serve:
cubes of toasted French bread
stalks of celery, trimmed
strips of red bell peppers

1 Rub the inside of a fondue pot with the cut clove of the garlic, then discard the garlic. Melt the butter in the pot on the stove, add the shallots and fry until soft. Add the mushrooms and fry for 2 minutes. Pour in the wine and heat gently until nearly boiling. Gradually add the cheeses, stirring continuously until melted.

2 Blend the cornstarch with the brandy and add to the pot, then stir until thickened. Add the cooked shrimp and cream and season with salt and pepper. Reduce the heat and cook for 3–4 minutes until heated through.

3 Transfer the fondue pot to the table and keep hot on a burner. Serve with cubes of toasted bread, celery, and strips of red bell pepper to dip into the fondue.

Serves 4
Preparation time: 10–15 minutes
Cooking time: 30–40 minutes

SEAFOOD AND WHITE WINE FONDUE

Use a wide fondue for this dish, similar to that used for making a cheese fondue.

12 ounces white fish fillet
¾ cup self-rising flour
generous pinch of salt
1 egg
⅔ cup water
oil, for deep-frying
chives, to garnish

Fondue:
5 tablespoons butter
½ cup all-purpose flour
1½ cups chicken stock
1¾ cups dry white wine
⅔ cup heavy cream
3 egg yolks
salt and pepper

To serve:
1 pound cooked and peeled
jumbo shrimp
cubes of hot French bread

1 Cut the fish fillet into ¼-inch cubes.

2 Sift the flour and salt into a bowl. Add the egg and a little of the water and beat until smooth. Beat in the remaining water.

3 Dip each piece of fish into the batter to give an even coating. Fill a deep pan one-third full with oil and heat on the stove to 375°F, or until a cube of bread browns in 30 seconds. Lower the fish into the hot oil and fry in batches for about 3 minutes until crisp and golden brown. Drain on paper towels. (The fish pieces can be prepared up to an hour in advance and then crisped up in a moderately hot oven.)

4 To make the fondue, melt the butter in a pan and stir in the flour. Cook for 1 minute, stirring. Gradually stir in the chicken stock and wine, whisking until the sauce is smooth. Season with salt and pepper to taste.

5 Transfer the wine sauce to the fondue pot and place over the burner to keep warm.

6 Beat the cream with the egg yolks and stir into the hot wine sauce – make sure that the fondue does not boil at this stage.

7 Divide the crispy fish pieces and shrimp between individual plates. Thread onto bamboo skewers or fondue forks and dip into the fondue. Accompany with cubes of hot French bread.

Serves 4
Preparation time: 25 minutes
Cooking time: 10–15 minutes

MUSSEL FONDUE

I garlic clove
⅔ cup dry white wine
4 cups grated Emmentaler cheese
I tablespoon cornstarch
I tablespoon parsley
I tablespoon dry sherry
I cup smoked mussels
salt and pepper
cubes of French bread, to serve

1 Rub the inside of a fondue pot with the cut garlic clove, then discard the garlic. Pour the wine into the pot and heat gently on the stove.

2 Gradually add the cheese and cornstarch, stirring continuously until all the cheese has melted. Stir in the parsley, sherry, and mussels. Season with salt and pepper and heat until thickened.

3 Transfer the fondue pot to the table and keep hot on a burner. Serve with cubes of French bread to dip into the fondue.

Serves 4
Preparation time: 10 minutes
Cooking time: 20 minutes

CRAB FONDUE

I garlic clove
1¼ cups dry white wine
10 ounces mild Cheddar cheese, grated
I tablespoon all-purpose flour
6 ounces white crab meat, flaked
salt and pepper
puff pastry crescents or cheese
straws, to serve

1 Rub the inside of a fondue pot with the cut garlic clove, then discard the garlic.

2 Pour the white wine into a fondue pot. Heat on the stove until the wine just reaches boiling point.

3 Mix the grated cheese with the flour and add to the hot wine, whisking or stirring until smooth. Season with salt and pepper and add the crab meat.

4 Transfer the fondue pot to the table and keep hot on a burner. Serve with crescents of puff pastry or cheese straws to dip.

Serves
Preparation time: 10 minutes
Cooking time: 10–15 minutes

MONGOLIAN LAMB HOT POT

2-pound piece frozen lamb fillet
2 ounces transparent noodles
1 large Chinese cabbage
1 pound spinach
2 blocks bean curd, thinly sliced
3 x 14½ ounce cans consommé

Dipping sauces:
6 green onions, finely chopped
2 tablespoons shredded fresh ginger root
4 tablespoons chopped cilantro
6 tablespoons sesame seed paste
3 tablespoons sesame seed oil
6 tablespoons soy sauce
4 tablespoons chile sauce

1 Allow the lamb to defrost slightly, but while it is still partially frozen, cut it into paper-thin slices, arrange them on a serving dish and allow to thaw completely.

2 Soak the noodles in hot water for 10 minutes; drain thoroughly.

3 Place the cabbage leaves and spinach on a serving dish. Arrange the bean curd and noodles on another dish.

4 To make the dipping sauces, combine the green onions and ginger in one bowl and garnish with cilantro. Mix the sesame seed paste and oil in another bowl. Put the soy sauce and chile sauce into individual bowls.

5 Heat the consommé in a saucepan on the stove until boiling. Carefully pour the consommé into a fondue pot, (or a Chinese Fondue, sometimes called a Shabu, as shown), and light the burner to keep hot.

6 Using chopsticks, fondue forks, or long skewers, each person dips a slice of meat into the hot consommé to cook for a few minutes, depending on desired doneness, then dips it into their chosen sauce before eating.

7 When you have eaten the meat, the vegetables, bean curd and noodles are added to the pot and cooked for about 5–10 minutes. Serve this soup at the end of the meal. Alternatively, cook the meat and vegetables together in the hot consommé and eat at once as a hearty soup.

Serves 4–6
Preparation time: 35 minutes
Cooking time: 10–15 minutes

CHINESE FONDUE

I quart chicken stock
I onion, thinly sliced
I large carrot, peeled and sliced
I stalk of celery, chopped
4 large mushrooms, sliced
3 slices fresh ginger root

To dip:
2½ cups tiny button mushrooms
I heart Chinese cabbage, shredded
½ small cauliflower, divided into tiny florets
I cup snow peas
I cup peeled shrimp
I cup boned chicken, cut into thin strips
6 ounces calves' liver, cut into thin strips
6 ounces fillet of beef, cut into thin strips
6 ounces pork fillet, cut into thin strips

To serve:
boiled rice or noodles
accompanying sauces (see right)

1 Put the stock into a saucepan with the onion, carrot, celery, mushrooms, and ginger. Simmer gently for 10 minutes.

2 Arrange the prepared mushrooms, cabbage, cauliflower, snow peas, shrimp, chicken, liver, beef, and pork decoratively on a platter, grouping them according to type.

3 Transfer the stock to the Chinese Fondue (Shabu) or fondue pot, and keep hot over a burner.

4 To serve, provide each person with bowls of different flavored sauces, and an accompanying bowl of rice or noodles.

Sauces for Chinese fondue:

Soy and garlic sauce:
Put ⅔ cup soy sauce into a pan with 3 finely chopped garlic cloves and simmer for 1–2 minutes. Serve warm or cold.

Plum sauce:
Mix 6 tablespoons plum jam with 2 tablespoons vinegar and 2 tablespoons chopped mango chutney. Serve cold. (If the jam is chunky, strain it). Alternatively, you can buy this sauce from Chinese stores and some supermarkets.

Green onion sauce:
Mix 6 tablespoons olive oil with 3 finely chopped green onions, 1 crushed garlic clove, 1 tablespoon sesame seeds, and salt and pepper to taste.

Lime and pepper sauce:
Mix the juice of 2 limes with 1 finely chopped red bell pepper, 1 finely chopped small onion, 3 tablespoons olive oil, and salt and pepper to taste.

Serves 4–6
Preparation time: 40 minutes
Cooking time: 10–15 minutes

PORK SATAY FONDUE

1½ pounds lean pork fillet
vegetable oil, for deep-frying
Satay sauce (see below), to serve

Marinade:
1¼ cups coconut milk
2 slices fresh ginger root
1 teaspoon ground coriander
1 teaspoon turmeric
1 teaspoon dark brown sugar
salt and pepper

1 Cut the meat into bite-sized pieces. Mix all the marinade ingredients together and marinate the meat overnight. Drain and dry on paper towels.
2 Pour sufficient oil to come about halfway up a fondue pot. Heat the oil on the stove to 375°F, or until a cube of bread browns in 30 seconds, then transfer the pot to the fondue burner to keep hot.
3 Serve each person with a portion of the meat. A piece of meat is then speared onto a fondue fork and placed in the hot oil until cooked. Serve with the sauce, for dipping.

Serves 4
Preparation time: 40 minutes, plus marinating
Cooking time: 5 minutes

SATAY SAUCE

2 onions
2 tablespoons oil
¾ cup roasted peanuts
½ teaspoon chili powder
⅔ cup warm water
1 tablespoon brown sugar
1–2 tablespoons soy sauce
juice of ½ lemon
salt

1 Slice 1 of the onions and fry in the oil. Roughly chop the second onion and place it in a blender or food processor with the peanuts and chili powder and blend until a paste is formed.
2 Add this paste to the fried onion and cook for a few minutes. Gradually stir in the water and sugar and cook for 2 minutes. Season to taste with salt, soy sauce, and lemon juice and heat through gently.

Serves 4
Preparation time: 10 minutes
Cooking time: about 12 minutes

MINIATURE SPRING ROLLS

¾ cup all-purpose flour
⅓ cup cornstarch
I egg
scant I cup water
oil, for deep-frying
I egg white, lightly beaten, for brushing
salt and pepper
green onion and red pepper curls, to garnish (optional)

Filling:
I cup cooked chicken, minced
I tablespoon soy sauce
4 Chinese cabbage leaves, finely shredded
3 green onions, finely chopped
4 canned water chestnuts, finely chopped

Sweet and sour sauce:
4 tablespoons red wine vinegar
4 tablespoons brown sugar
I¼ cups chicken stock
I tablespoon tomato purée
2 teaspoons soy sauce
2 tablespoons cornstarch

I Sift the flour, the cornstarch and ½ teaspoon of salt into a bowl. Make a well in the center. Add the egg and a little of the water and beat to a paste. Gradually whisk in the remaining water.

2 To make the filling, mix together the chicken, soy sauce, cabbage, green onions, chestnuts, and salt and pepper to taste.

3 Brush a small 5-inch omelet or pancake pan with a little oil. Add 1 tablespoon of the batter and tilt the pan to give a thin, even layer. Cook the pancake for about 1 minute until the underside is just brown, then turn over and cook for 15 seconds, and place on a greased tray.

4 Continue with the remaining batter until you have made about 12–14 small pancakes.

5 Lay the pancakes flat, and place a spoonful of the filling in the middle of each pancake. Brush the outer edge of each pancake with a little beaten egg white.

6 Roll up the pancakes, tucking the ends in firmly, sealing them with a little more beaten egg white if necessary. (The prepared pancakes can be chilled at this stage until needed.)

7 To make the sauce, put all the ingredients except for the cornstarch into a pan and bring to the boil. Mix the cornstarch with 3 tablespoons cold water and stir into the hot liquid. Return the sauce to the pan and stir over a moderate heat until smooth.

8 Fill the fondue pot one-third full with oil and heat on the stove to 375°F, or until a cube of bread browns in 30 seconds. Carefully transfer the fondue pot to the table and keep hot on a burner. Carefully lower 2–3 spring rolls at a time into the hot oil and deep-fry for 2–3 minutes until crisp and golden.

9 Provide each person with a plate covered with greaseproof paper or paper towels, and a small bowl of sauce. Garnish with green onion and red pepper curls if liked.

Note: Cut the green onions and peppers into small strips and place in a bowl of iced water for about 1 hour, or until curled.

Serves 4–6
Preparation time: 30 minutes
Cooking time: about 1 hour

MARINATED PORK IN ORANGE FONDUE

1½ pounds lean pork fillet
1 teaspoon cornstarch
1 tablespoon water
vegetable oil, for deep-frying
salt and pepper

Marinade:
grated zest and juice of 1 orange
1 garlic clove, crushed
⅔ cup apple juice
2 tablespoons oil
1 teaspoon soft brown sugar

1 Cut the meat into bite-sized pieces. Mix all the marinade ingredients together and marinate the meat for a few hours or preferably overnight. Drain, reserving the marinade, and dry on paper towels.
2 Pour the marinade into a saucepan and bring to the boil. Blend the cornstarch with the water, stir into the sauce and simmer for 2 minutes. Season with salt and pepper to taste.
3 Fill a fondue pot one-third full with oil and heat on the stove to 375°F, or until a cube of bread browns in 30 seconds. Carefully transfer the fondue pot to the table and keep hot on a burner.
4 Spear a piece of meat onto a fondue fork and cook it in the hot oil until cooked to your liking. Serve the hot marinade sauce with the fondue as a dipping sauce.

Serves 4
Preparation time: 20–30 minutes, plus marinating
Cooking time: 10 minutes

SPICY MEATBALL FONDUE

1 tablespoon sunflower oil
1 onion, finely chopped
1 pound extra lean ground beef
¼ teaspoon grated nutmeg
¼ teaspoon garlic salt
1 egg, beaten
flour, for shaping
oil, for frying
salt and pepper

To serve:
barbecue sauce
green salad

1 Heat the sunflower oil in a frying pan, add the onion and fry until softened. Leave to cool slightly and then mix with the beef, nutmeg, garlic salt, egg, and salt and pepper to taste. With well-floured hands shape the mixture into small balls.
2 Half-fill a fondue pot with oil and heat on the stove to 375°F, or until a cube of bread browns in 30 seconds.
3 Carefully place the pot over a fondue burner. Spear each meatball with a long fondue fork and cook in the hot oil for 3–4 minutes or until browned. Serve with barbecue sauce and a green salad.

Serves 4–6
Preparation time: 20 minutes
Cooking time: 5–10 minutes

ROSEMARY LAMB FONDUE

If you like, the marinade can be heated, thickened with cornstarch, and served with the fondue.

1½ pounds fillet of lamb
vegetable oil, for deep-frying

Marinade:
1 garlic clove, crushed
⅔ cup red wine
2 tablespoons chopped fresh rosemary
1 tablespoon redcurrant jelly
3 tablespoons oil
Cumberland Sauce (see below), to serve

1 Cut the lamb into bite-sized pieces. Mix all the marinade ingredients and pour into a large bowl. Add the lamb and mix thoroughly, then cover and leave to marinate overnight in the refrigerator. Drain and dry on paper towels; if the meat is wet it will cause the oil to spit when cooking.
2 Half-fill a fondue pot with oil and heat on the stove to 375°F, or until a cube of bread browns in 30 seconds. Then carefully transfer to the burner. Keep the oil hot. Serve each person with a portion of the lamb. Each person can then cook their lamb in the hot oil; the length of time depends on how rare or well done each person prefers their meat. Serve with the sauce.

Serves 4
Preparation time: 25 minutes, plus marinating
Cooking time: 5 minutes

CUMBERLAND SAUCE

1 orange
1 lemon
1 cup redcurrant jelly
6 tablespoons red wine
2 tablespoons brown sugar
1 teaspoon arrowroot
salt and pepper

1 Thinly remove the zest, without the pith, from the orange and the lemon. Shred the zest finely and place in a saucepan of boiling water for 3 minutes. Drain and immerse the zest in cold water for 1 minute. Drain again and set aside.
2 Squeeze the juice from the fruit, strain into a saucepan with the jelly and bring to the boil over a low heat. Stir in the wine, sugar, and salt and pepper to taste. Blend the arrowroot with a little cold water and stir into the sauce. Bring to the boil, stirring, until slightly thickened. Stir in the blanched citrus zest and serve.

Serves 4
Preparation time: 10–15 minutes
Cooking time: 10–15 minutes

FONDUE BOURGUIGNONNE

2 pounds fillet steak
vegetable oil, for deep-frying
sprigs of parsley or lettuce, to garnish

To serve:
accompanying sauces (see below)
French bread
green salad

1 Cut the fillet steak into ½–1 inch cubes. Season with salt and pepper to taste.

2 Add sufficient oil to half-fill a fondue pot. Heat the oil on the stove to 375°F, or until a cube of bread browns in 30 seconds, then carefully transfer to the fondue burner.

3 Provide each person with a plate of steak (about ½ pound per person), a fondue fork for spearing and cooking the steak; and a knife and fork for eating the meat.

4 Each person can then cook their steak in the hot oil for about 1–3 minutes. The length of time depends on how rare or well done each person prefers their meat.

5 Provide a selection of sauces for dipping, sprigs of parsley or lettuce to garnish, a basket of hot French bread, and a bowl of green salad.

Sauces:
Salsa verde:
In a blender process 2 tablespoons capers, 4 dill pickles, 2 garlic cloves, 4 tablespoons olive oil, 4 tablespoons white wine vinegar, 2 tablespoons fresh parsley, a pinch of sugar, and salt and pepper to taste.

Horseradish sauce:
Mix together 1 tablespoon grated fresh horseradish, the juice of ½ lemon, a pinch of sugar, ⅔ cup sour cream, and salt and pepper to taste.

Mustard sauce:
Mix together 1 finely chopped small onion, ⅔ cup mayonnaise, 1 tablespoon French mustard, ½ teaspoon cayenne pepper, and salt to taste.

Serves 4
Preparation time: about 10–15 minutes, plus making sauces
Cooking time: 5 minutes

BANANA FONDUE

3 bananas
1 tablespoon lemon juice
1 tablespoon sugar
5 tablespoons light cream
2 ounces dark chocolate, grated

To serve:
balls or slices of melon
chunks of pineapple

1 Blend the bananas in a food processor or blender, or push them through a sieve with the back of a metal spoon. Place in a fondue pot with the lemon juice and heat gently. Add the sugar and cream and, when simmering, gradually add the chocolate.
2 Once the chocolate has melted serve with balls or slices of melon and chunks of pineapple to dip into the fondue.

Serves 2
Preparation time: 10 minutes
Cooking time: 5–10 minutes

APRICOT FONDUE

3 cups dried or glazed apricots
1 cup sugar
pinch of cinnamon
4 tablespoons apricot brandy

To serve:
cubes of pound cake or sponge cake (see page 57)
wafer cookies

1 Soak the apricots until soft, then simmer them in a little water until tender. Pureé the apricots in a blender or food processor.
2 Place the apricot pureé in a fondue pot. Add the sugar, cinnamon and a little water if the mixture is very thick. Heat gently, then stir in the apricot brandy before serving.
3 Transfer the fondue pot to the table and keep warm on the burner. Serve with cubes of pound cake or sponge cake and cookies to dip into the fondue.

Serves 2–4
Preparation time: 10 minutes, plus soaking
Cooking time: 20 minutes

CHOCOLATE ORANGE FONDUE

8 ounces dark chocolate, broken into pieces
1 tablespoon butter
finely grated zest and juice of 1 orange
1 teaspoon arrowroot
2 tablespoons Cointreau or other orange liqueur

To serve:
macaroons
almond cookies
segments of clementines or oranges

1 Place the chocolate, butter, and orange zest and juice in a fondue pot and heat gently, stirring continuously, until the chocolate has just melted.

2 Blend the arrowroot with the Cointreau and add to the fondue pot, stirring until thickened.

3 Serve with macaroons, almond cookies, and segments of clementine or orange speared onto fondue forks or bamboo sticks to dip into the fondue.

Serves 2
Preparation time: 10 minutes
Cooking time: 10 minutes

BLACKCURRANT CREAM FONDUE

1 cup blackcurrants, trimmed
½ cup sugar
½ cup butter
¾ cup plus 1 tablespoon water
1 tablespoon cornstarch
⅔ cup heavy cream
biscotti or almond cookies, to serve

1 Place the blackcurrants, sugar, butter, and ¾ cup water in a saucepan and allow the sugar to dissolve over a low heat.

2 Bring to the boil and simmer until the blackcurrants are soft. Allow to cool slightly then strain the fruit.

3 Blend the cornstarch with the 1 tablespoon of water. Pour the fruit purée into a fondue pot and stir in the cornstarch mixture. Bring to the boil, stirring, and simmer for 2 minutes. Add the cream. Reheat gently, stirring constantly, but do not allow to boil. Serve with Italian biscotti or almond cookies to dip into the fondue or spoon the warm fondue over the cookies on your plate.

Serves 4
Preparation time: 10 minutes
Cooking time: 20 minutes

RASPBERRY MALLOW FONDUE

1½ cups raspberries, fresh or frozen
1 x 6-ounce package marshmallows
⅔ cup heavy cream
few drops of lemon juice

To serve:
wafer cookies
macaroons

1 Defrost the raspberries if frozen. Blend in a blender until they are puréed.
2 Place the raspberry purée, marshmallows, and cream in a fondue pot and allow to melt over a low heat, stirring constantly.
3 Add the lemon juice and reheat, but do not allow to boil. Serve with wafer cookies and macaroons.

Serves 4
Preparation time: 5 minutes
Cooking time: 5–10 minutes

FRUIT AND CHOCOLATE FONDUE

½ cup heavy cream
8 ounces semisweet chocolate, finely chopped
I teaspoon vanilla extract

To serve:
cubes of pound cake (see below)
strawberries
slices of fresh or glazed apricot

I Fill the fondue pot one-third full with water. Place the porcelain bowl insert in the pot and heat on the stove. (Alternatively, place a heatproof bowl over a saucepan of gently simmering water.) Put the cream in the bowl and heat gently. As soon as the cream starts to bubble around the edges, turn off the heat and whisk in the chocolate. When the chocolate has melted, add the vanilla and stir well to mix.
2 Transfer the fondue to the table and keep warm on the burner.
3 Serve with the cubes of pound cake, strawberries, and slices of apricot. Use fondue forks, toothpicks or bamboo sticks to dip the cake and fruit into the chocolate fondue.

Serves 6–8
Preparation time: 10–15 minutes
Cooking time: 5–10 minutes

POUND CAKE

I½ cups all-purpose flour
½ teaspoon baking powder
I cup butter
I¼ cups sugar
4 eggs

I Lightly grease and flour a 4½ x 8½ x 3-inch loaf pan. Sift the flour and baking powder together and set aside.
2 Cream the butter and sugar together in a bowl until light and fluffy. Add the eggs, one at a time, beating well after each egg. Add 1 tablespoon of flour if the mixture starts to curdle.
3 Fold in the flour and pour into the loaf pan. Bake in a preheated oven, at 350°F, for about 45 minutes until golden. To test if the cake is done, insert a toothpick into the center of the cake. The cake is ready if the toothpick comes out clean.
4 Cool for 10 minutes in the pan; then turn onto a wire rack to cool completely before serving.

Serves 6–8
Preparation time: 20 minutes
Cooking time: 45 minutes

NUTTY DARK CHOCOLATE FONDUE

1 x 3½-ounce bar Toblerone chocolate
2 ounces dark chocolate
2 tablespoons heavy cream
1 tablespoon rum

To serve:
selection of fruit including strawberries,
raspberries, red and white cherries,
and sliced banana
cookies

1 Fill the fondue pot one-third full with water. Place the porcelain bowl insert in the pot and heat on the stove. (Alternatively, place a heatproof bowl over a saucepan of gently simmering water.) Break all the chocolate into the porcelain bowl and add the cream. Stir until the chocolate has melted. Stir in the rum and continue to heat, stirring, for 1 minute.

2 Transfer the fondue to the table and keep warm over the burner. Serve with a selection of fruits and cookies for dipping, using bamboo skewers or toothpicks to spear the fruit or simply dip them by their stems.

Serves 4
Preparation time: 15 minutes
Cooking time: 10 minutes

WHITE CHOCOLATE FONDUE

9 ounces white chocolate
½ cup heavy cream
1 tablespoon Kirsch

To serve:
strawberries
kiwi fruit

1 Heat the chocolate and cream in a fondue pot, stirring continuously, but do not boil. When melted, stir in the Kirsch.

2 Transfer the fondue pot to the table and keep warm over the burner. Serve with strawberries and chunks of kiwi fruit, using bamboo skewers or toothpicks to spear the fruit.

Serves 2
Preparation time: 5–10 minutes
Cooking time: 10 minutes

CHOCOLATE MINT FONDUE

1 pound dark chocolate, grated
4 tablespoons crème de menthe
or mint chocolate liqueur
⅔ cup heavy cream

To serve:
raspberries
slices of banana
chocolate mints

1 Place the chocolate in a fondue pot and allow to melt over a low heat. Stir in the liqueur and cream and reheat gently, stirring continuously. Do not allow to boil.

2 Transfer the fondue pot to the table and keep warm over the burner. Serve with raspberries, slices of banana, and chocolate mints. Provide bamboo skewers or toothpicks to spear the fruit.

Serves 6
Preparation time: 10 minutes
Cooking time: 10 minutes

ICE CREAM FONDUE

1 pint coffee ice cream
1 tablespoon brandy
1 tablespoon cornstarch

To serve:
chunks of banana
lemon juice, for sprinkling
chocolate sticks

1 Melt the ice cream in the fondue pot. Mix the brandy and cornstarch and stir into the pot.
2 Serve with chunks of banana sprinkled with lemon juice and chocolate sticks to dip into the fondue.

Serves 2
Preparation time: 10 minutes
Cooking time: 5 minutes

DARK FUDGE FONDUE

2 tablespoons butter
6 tablespoons dark brown sugar
¾ cup milk
1 tablespoon molasses
1 tablespoon cornstarch blended
with 3 tablespoons water

To serve:
vanilla wafers and a selection of cookies
marshmallows

1 Place the butter and sugar in a saucepan and heat gently until the sugar dissolves. Bring to the boil and simmer for 1 minute, stirring well.
2 Add the milk, molasses, and blended cornstarch and water. Bring to the boil, stirring continuously, then simmer gently for 2–3 minutes.
3 Transfer to a fondue pot and keep warm over a burner. Serve with vanilla wafers, a selection of plain cookies, and marshmallows to dip into the fondue.

Serves 2
Preparation time: 10 minutes
Cooking time: 10 minutes

MOCHA FONDUE

1 pound dark chocolate
2 tablespoons instant coffee granules
1½ cups heavy cream
2 tablespoons sherry

To serve:
1 x 6-ounce package marshmallows
pound cake (see page 57)

1 Grate the chocolate and mix with the coffee granules.

2 Place the cream in a porcelain or heatproof bowl and add the chocolate and coffee. Place over the fondue pot half-filled with simmering water and heat gently, stirring continuously until the chocolate is thoroughly blended and smooth.

3 Stir in the sherry and heat gently, then transfer to the table and place over a fondue burner to keep warm.

4 Serve with marshmallows or cubes of pound cake to dip into the fondue.

Serves 4
Preparation time: 10 minutes
Cooking time: 10–15 minutes

INDEX